WE TALKED ABOUT NEW YORK

OTHER BOOKS BY KLECKO

A Bakeable Feast
Zelda's Bed
The Dead Fitzgeralds
3 a.m. Austin Texas
Lincolnland
Hitman-Baker-Casketmaker:
Aftermath of an American's Clash with ICE
Out for a Lark
The Bluebeard of Happiness
A Pox Upon Your Blessings
Houdini in St. Paul
My British Hindu Bible
Robert Bly and the Monk in His Cell
Mayor 4 Life
Brando Land

Winner of the 2020 Midwest Book Award for *Hitman-Baker-Casketmaker: Aftermath of an American's Clash with ICE*

Longlisted for Best Independent Book of 2021 by *Shelf Unbound*
Regular contributor to The New York Times

PRAISE FOR KLECKO

"In Klecko's personal, powerful collection of poems, he grapples with his feelings on a variety of topics including baseball, family and the fallout of a U.S. Immigration and Customs Enforcement Audit."
—Tim Carman, *Washington Post*

"Klecko's affection for his crew spill out onto the pages."
—Lee Svitak Dean, *Star Tribune*

"Klecko has become an ambassador for both poetry and immigrant issues."
—Nancy Weingartner, *Food Service News*

"People in the industry know that bakers tend to be a spiritual lot. One of our most philosophical has to be the St. Paul baker that goes by one name: Klecko. He's written for years about the industry and baking life for different publications, but his new work is very personal, and important."
—Stephanie March, *Mpls. St. Paul Magazine*

"Energetic host of readings as well as writing, Klecko is one of his own biggest fans. As he puts it, 'This is the most important book about hospitality since Anthony Bourdain's *Kitchen Confidential.*'"
—Mary Ann Grossmann, *St.Paul Pioneer Press*

WE TALKED ABOUT NEW YORK

KLECKO

PARIS MORNING
PUBLICATIONS

Published in 2025 by Paris Morning Publications
www.parismorningpublications.com

Published and reprinted in the United States of America
ISBN: 979-8-218-47744-8
Book design by Mayfly book design
Cover design by Audrey Campbell
www.ataudrey.com

DEDICATION

For Isabella

INTRODUCTION #1

Mary Ann Grossmann is in her 80s, she's a beautiful vegetarian feminist who has been writing book reviews for the Saint Paul Pioneer Press for over 60 years. Many in the Capital City would have you believe she is the best Minnesota has to offer. I think that's selling her short; in my opinion Grossmann is a national treasure.

When the pandemic came to its conclusion, Grossmann tagged along with me and my publisher as we drove to Duluth to fly kites with novelist Leif Enger. During the two-and-a-half-hour commute, my publisher and I were entertained by stories of Grossmann being playfully kidnapped by Studs Terkel to be his date at some kind of nautical party on Lake Minnetonka. When the story began to fade, I asked Grossmann if there had been a love connection. I asked her if she put out.

"A woman never tells."

She said this before switching gears and telling us about the time Susan Sontag came to the Twin Cities to accept an award or give a lecture, either way, there was a point when Grossmann was alone with Sontag in a hotel room. Conversation was sparse and Grossmann began feeling as if she was failing in her hosting responsibilities, so to pass time Grossmann explained to Sontag that we were in the midst of our state fair and if Sontag wanted, Grossmann would take her over to view the world's largest pig.

Sontag declined.

My publisher and Grossmann switched gears once again and began talking about authors they liked. I occasionally interrupted and mentioned writers I hated.

Eventually Grossmann resumed control of the conversation and began a rant where she stated that 99% of all authors waste the first page of their books. When I asked her to explain, she said something to the effect that all opening pages are the same. They all open with descriptions of sky or water. I began laughing and paraphrased the opening page in a Jane Goodall book where she described the jungle's treetops being welded to the skyline.

Grossmann chuckled and reminded us that if Goodall was capable of botching an opening, things didn't bode well for the rest of us. Finally, I asked if anyone in the history of literature had ever produced a great opening page. I'm pretty sure Grossmann anticipated this question. Without hesitation she responded:

"*Lonesome Dove* by Larry McMurtry, what a great book, what an opening page. I'm sure you've read it, right? How those two blue pigs play tug-of-war with that rattlesnake."

I could go on and on, telling you stories and clever quips that have been exchanged between Grossmann and America's literary elite, but truthfully, more interesting than that is her commitment to local writers, in our case Minnesota writers.

For over half a century, Grossmann has anchored all things book-related for the Pioneer Press, while her rival across the river, that paper in Babylon, whose name I won't even mention, utilizes a staff of employees who commit more column space to stories about its editors' dogs instead of promoting homegrown talent. Grossmann does the opposite, she goes it alone, always finding the pertinent story before it breaks, always making sure to encourage and promote the writers of her region.

The reason I bring this up is because a couple of weeks ago Grossmann and I were on the phone. At one point she asked what my next book was going to be. I mentioned several ideas I was considering, but these options were met with silence.

Once the quiet surpassed awkward, I asked if my ideas were droll. Grossmann answered my question with a question;

"Don't you think you should be writing about New York?"

INTRODUCTION #2

Patricia Hampl is a memoirist, writer, lecturer and educator. Before retiring she taught in the MFA program at the University of Minnesota and is one of the founding members of the Loft Literary Center.

If Saint Paul made a Mount Rushmore sculpture, showcasing the Capital City's top four writers, Trish would be a natural selection.

Mary Ann Grossmann once told me that the thing she most admires about Hampl is that when her career was at its peak, the natural thing to do would have been to move to New York. The move would have been logical, if not beneficial, but Hampl didn't. She stayed put in Saint Paul.

One winter when she tripped and broke her shoulder, I stopped by frequently to shovel and make sure she was fine. Sometimes there was tea involved, other times wine, but every time, somewhere in our conversation she would tell me things about writers. She loves Fitzgerald the most, but that didn't mean she didn't gush over others.

Brenda Ueland, Fredrick Manfred, Meridel Le Sueur, Garrison Keillor, Sinclair Lewis and Robert Bly . . . the list went on and on.

Over the last few years, when I'm about to embark on a project, more often than not, I run it by Hampl. That's why after I got the suggestion from Grossmann to write about New York, I called Trish to tell her.

With little comment, she agreed with Grossmann and asked me for a brief plot outline. Before I found a way to articulate potential themes, Trish asked if I would consider doing something like E.B. White did with *Here Is New York*.

Truthfully, I was a bit embarrassed. She had mentioned the author and the book as if they were household names, but I'd never heard of them. When I confessed this, Trish took down my mailing address and told me she'd have a copy to me in less than 24 hours.

INTRODUCTION #3

I received *Here Is New York*.

I read it 80 years after its publication, and I loved it.

E.B. White took us into deep dives where we learned the greatest thing New York City has to offer is anonymity.

He also taught us there are three groups of people who inhabit New York City.

Those who are born there and take it for granted, daily commuters and dreamers who arrive with manuscripts and a belief they are luckier than their competition.

There's another group, a fourth group that E.B.White forgot.

Poets.

INTRODUCTION #4

To be a successful poet
You only have to follow two rules
#1 – Observe
#2 – Love
It's really that simple
If you are a poet
If you follow these rules
The fish will jump into the boat

45 MINUTES IN CENTRAL PARK

(New York Times – Feb.12, 2023)

Between the hours of 9 and 10
On a bench adjacent to mine
Sat a man who was not put together
A man in the grip of some battle
Big drops of rain began to fall
Raindrops by the tablespoon
The man refused to move
A woman with a terrier
Stopped as if she knew him
Offering dry comfort
Underneath her umbrella
The man began to cry
What determines luck, who makes up the rules
Why is value attached to everything but me
The woman sat by his side
Put her arm around his shoulder
In silence the umbrella twirled
Until she offered explanation
Everything will be fine she said
Just not today

OBSERVATION ON THE D - LINE

(New York Times – June 4, 2023)

5:23 p.m.
Five boys sat apart
With no regard for posture
Slumping in their seats
Afraid to look away from their video games
5:30
Two angry women sat together
Both had greasy hair
They might have been swearing in Korean
When melons escaped their grocery bags
5:36
A woman across the aisle
Stared and called me tourist
When I asked how she knew
She mentioned I was smiling
5:38
Then she told me she was sad
But how sad she couldn't determine
Her chest kept getting in the way
Making it impossible to tell
If her heart was bruised or broken

CELEBRATING WHITMAN

(New York Times – Dec.17, 2023)

(1)

It was 96 degrees, and carousel music was playing
As I approached the academics who were hosting
The annual Walt Whitman celebration
At Brooklyn Bridge Park
I asked if there was room for another reader
And was told to talk to the woman in blue
She was a literary professor and had the final say
When I talked to the woman in blue
She said participants needed to have registered online
I wanted to read, so I told the truth
I'm kind of a big deal, I said
Your audience will love me
With a look of uncertainty, she handed me the mic
And with the Brooklyn Bridge as a backdrop
I borrowed a book from a woman
Who was standing there as I faced the audience
And sounded out my barbaric yawp

CELEBRATING WHITMAN

(2)
"Sometimes with one I love
I fill myself with rage for fear
I effuse unreturned love
But now I think there is no unreturned love
The pay is certain one way or the other
I loved a certain person ardently
And my love was not returned
Yet out of that, I have written these songs."
As I bowed and begun to take my leave
People cheered
As I exited the stage
I realized for the first time
What it felt like to be absolved

CHESS IN BRYANT PARK—PREQUEL

[To my friends from the Lee Summit Chess Club]

Today at the park, I made a new friend
His name was Moses
He plays chess for money
I offered to play two-minute clocks
Moses insisted on five minutes
I held firm
He smiled
We played
He gave me white
I opened with an Alapin variation
As pieces were exchanged at a rapid pace
Moses kept saying . . .
That's it, that's it, sir
About 75 seconds in, I hung my queen
For a moment, I was in shock
After resigning, my friend Moses said . . .
Don't worry, if you want
We can play again

CHESS IN BRYANT PARK

(New York Times – June 16, 2024)

On a day less wet
I was inclined to finance a rematch
I felt good
Pieces landed on the proper squares
I felt good
Giving my combatant reason to pause
But in the end, I was going up against
A champion
A legend
I was going up against
Moses
A man who when asked
When is the last time you lost
Smiled kindness
While softly saying
It's been a while
I can't quite remember

FLOAT (REVISED)

(New York Times – Sept. 29, 2024)

I was at that place in Central Park
That place replicated to look like Paris
Where people came to sail model boats
A kid eating ice cream handed me a remote control
Urging me to cast off
Zoom – Zoom, how relaxing
Zoom – Zoom, feel the glide
Ice cream kid asked
If I could sail anywhere in the world
Where would I go
I answered that I'd like to go to England
Ice cream kid replied
If you get to go anywhere
It's best to go someplace with a volcano
After thinking about it
I didn't disagree

ALBERTINE BOOKS
(New York Times – Jan.12, 2025)

What do I know about France
What do I know about French bookstores in NYC
Not much is the answer to both questions
But I do know about sisters, and I saw two sisters
In a French bookstore, it's not like I asked them
Are you sisters, I didn't need to
I could tell by watching them amidst a dispute
When sisters have conflict, their reactions are unique
Sister #1 said something I couldn't hear
Sister #2 replied . . . In Malaysia people don't mention
The tiger for fear it will draw him out
I'm not sure if this was an allegory
But for a moment, the moment became sharp
But coincidentally in a moment, after that moment
The sisters hugged each other with their eyes
While allowing each other red carpets of retreat
I didn't end up buying a French book
Instead, I considered sisters
Before leaving in pursuit of ice cream

NOTES ON 45 MINUTES IN CENTRAL PARK

(1)
Unless something strange happens
"45 Minutes in Central Park" will end up being
The most popular poem I will ever write
The piece came into existence
During my first-ever trip to New York City
I had just finished a cookbook
And Martha Stewart Radio
Wanted me to appear in studio
After my flight was booked
After my hotel was booked
After doing the math
I realized I had 22 hours in Manhattan
I decided this might be
The type of excursion
To embark on with a guest
So, I invited the Canadian to join me
The Canadian said yes

NOTES ON 45 MINUTES IN CENTRAL PARK

(2)
We touched down at the airport at 5 p.m.
After getting settled in
After a Cajun dinner
After Russian cocktails
We returned to the hotel
Well past midnight
We needed to be in studio at 6 a.m.
We only had three hours to sleep
After the interview
We only had seven hours to explore
Before returning to the airport
Our remaining itinerary was mapped out
On a small notebook
Kept by the Canadian

NOTES ON 45 MINUTES IN CENTRAL PARK

(3)
Everything left to do
Was marked off in 15-minute increments
I remember walking down busy sidewalks
I remember the Canadian saying to me
Look at how fit all these people are
Look how handsome they all are
It would appear that only those
Blessed with sparkling genetics
Make this their stomping ground
Then just like that . . .
Our path was blocked
The street was blocked
People and people beyond that
Stood by and around several trailers
Some pointed cameras
Others goose-necked
Everybody gawked
The Canadian asked nobody in particular
What gives, what's all the fuss about

NOTES ON 45 MINUTES IN CENTRAL PARK

(4)
Nobody in particular responded
It's been reported
Jennifer Lopez and Ben Affleck
Are in one of those trailers
They are here shooting a film
(*Maid in Manhattan*)
We're just hanging out to catch a glimpse
The Canadian asked this new friend
How long have you been waiting
The new friend answered
Two hours
Tick – Tock, time was ticking
Tick – Tock, the Canadian smiled
While informing me
Let's give it five minutes
If nothing happens
We'll scram
Nothing happened

NOTES ON 45 MINUTES IN CENTRAL PARK

(5)

The crescendo of our experience came

As we stood at the entrance of Central Park

The Canadian announced

We have 45 minutes

After that we have to head to the airport

I thought about that

How much can you see

In less than an hour

My highlight was what I wrote

In the poem

Which years later

I would send off to The New York Times

It was accepted

And the exposure it received

I received

Changed things in my poetry existence

MORE NOTES ON 45 MINUTES IN CENTRAL PARK

(1)
The first book I published
Was *K-9 Nation Biscuit Book*
A series of dog biscuit recipes
My first tour stop in support of this book
Was NYC, Martha Stewart Radio
That was my first trip to the Big Apple
I was excited, I was nervous
The night before I left, I went to the home
Of my writing coach "Big Vanilla"
After listening to the coastal antics of his youth
We drank bottles of red
As I was about to leave, my friend hugged me
And handed me an envelope
He didn't mention what it contained
Or how valuable its contents were
I found out the following day
As I buckled up, and my jet taxied toward takeoff
This was an appropriate time
To open the envelope and view its contents
A message of encouragement
The letter read . . .

MORE NOTES ON 45 MINUTES IN CENTRAL PARK

(2)
"When I was in LaGuardia, it was 70 degrees
All I needed was a jacket, for three days I walked the streets
Leery of beggars who seem to know something
While shadowy figures lurked in doorways
But the temperature began to fall
And the canyon gusts lifted plastic sacks
Like ghostly luggage
I came into my own
I am more used to winter than them
It is my element
As I walked in the wind along 6th Avenue
Muggers and murderers parted
Melted from their purpose by sled dog eyes
Urgent and cheerful on a cold – cold night"

BIG PINK BUS

Somewhere between drip – drip – drip
And pitter patter, I climbed aboard
A pink double-decker bus
With 73 women ranging in age
Size and level of kindness displayed
For 90 minutes we circled Manhattan
Taking in the sights while enjoying High Tea
While a good-looking gal
Good looking in an evangelical way
A born-again way
An Amy Grant way
Sang us standards over a microphone
Hallelujah . . . we ate scones
Hallelujah . . . we drank tea
While I traded finger sandwiches
Egg salad for cucumber
At a glacial pace we toured the metro
While the tea attendant
With the well-manicured beard
Reminded us few things are better
Than stumbling onto a warm beverage
That reminds you of Fruit Loops

PARKING LOT GREAT

A certain thing won't make you great
A certain attitude will
On a plane, if you are flying alone
Never talk to strangers seated next to you
Once you open that door
Most people won't let you close it
If you are lonely, in need of conversation
Find a venue that offers escape
Recently I was in a parking lot
One of those lots where they stack cars
I was bored – I was lonely
Not far from me stood a guy, staring ahead, smoking
He raised his hands, swung his arms
Like a maniac or Bob Fosse
He said . . . Look across the asphalt
Notice the broken glass and garbage
Create an artful image
Complete with texture and perspective
A certain thing won't make you great
A certain decision will
I walked away from cigarette man
With the understanding
Our worlds had no need to collide

HOTEL – NYC

(1)
In a cock-eyed world or an old hotel
Voices sound funny
Not the tone as much as the content
There were two chairs off the lobby
In a room that neglected
To state obvious purpose
There were two chairs off the lobby
Perhaps a place to observe
Small gestures in a big city
There were two chairs off the lobby
Occupied by a man and a woman
In a cock-eyed world or an old hotel
The man stared forward into nothing
Itemizing things of importance
Dire things

HOTEL - NYC

(2)
He quivered – He mumbled
She fidgeted and began talking
To herself or to no one in particular
Something about Etsy
Or possibly Pinterest
It didn't matter, what did matter
Was the man in the chair
Smiled with a look that clearly stated
He had found an answer
The answer that had evaded him, he said . . .
The Christmas tree has been up 122 days
That's over a third of the year
That's not normal behavior
You do realize that, don't you
The woman thought about it
Just for a moment before answering . . .
I like the lights
They are pretty
No?

ALIVE AT THE ALGONQUIN

J.F.K. once said . . .
When growing up, I had three wishes
I wanted to be a Lindbergh-type hero
Learn Chinese, and become a member of
The Algonquin Round Table
Dust in the wind – You are dead, Jack
Dust in the wind – As are the Round Table founders
Dust in the wind – But . . . I am alive
Conquering New York City
Amidst an unprecedented entourage
Sissy, Bama & Moses
Filled with breath, touched by grace
Filled with breath, immersed in joy
Filming poems in Times Square
Receiving reprimand at the Plaza
Hanging your queen in Bryant Park
Filming poems at Washington Square Park
Amidst junkies and interpretive dance

DEAD ALI

Stepping out of Tavern on the Green
A long-haired man, dressed like a chimney sweep
Made mention of my Muhammad Ali tattoo
Once the doorman realized I wasn't local
He encouraged me to visit Jimmy's Corner
A boxing-themed bar not far from Times Square
The doorman told me Jimmy's Corner was legendary
You never knew who would drop in
But even if famous fighters didn't surface
Something unexplainable always seemed to happen there
Later that evening, I took the doorman's advice
And headed over, hoping I might have a drink
In the presence of a heavyweight champion
Hours passed, nothing eventful, nothing unusual
I found this hard to believe, the doorman seemed so certain
Eventually I returned to my hotel room
Where I tried to douse my disappointment
With whiskey and Yankees baseball
Within moments I nodded off, but at a moment
Equally distanced between sunset and sunrise
I woke up to a glowing television
In the midst of announcing
Muhammad Ali had died

45 MINUTES IN WASHINGTON SQUARE PARK

Somewhere between thunder and memory
The heavens opened and the flood began
Rising water served no purpose
To a multitude of junkies strung out
I took refuge under the arch, but found myself
Sharing space with a handful of do-gooders
Who believed they could best serve our planet
And themselves by handing out pamphlets
Which of course were soggy by now
Across the way, in the middle of the plaza
A woman danced to eerie music
Music that seemed to haunt with intention
Somewhere between thunder and memory
I remembered the moment we stood there
In sunshine, away from the slaughter
But that was then, and this was now
One of the few places where I've felt defeated
One of the few places where poetry didn't matter
The woman danced and danced, as if her movements
Were specifically choreographed to serve as a magnet
Meant to gather those bent on self-destruction
The obvious choice seemed simple, get out
But oddly enough, I didn't know how to proceed

ANOTHER CASSIDY OPERA

(1)
Houdini, you're dead and I am alive
And for that reason, I made plans
To visit your grave
I even brought a magic rock
From Lake Superior
I intended to place it on your tombstone
But you know how it goes, Harry
Consideration and consequences
I never made it to Brooklyn
Houdini, you're dead and I am alive
And I hope – And I hope
And I hope so much
That you'll pardon my absence
With the realization that this time
It wasn't in the cards

ANOTHER CASSIDY OPERA

(2)
In second grade, through a cracked door
I heard the guidance counselor tell my mother
We don't think he's retarded, but . . .
As she closed the door completely
It left me to wonder if this announcement
Should cause shame or relief
Next, they ran a battery of tests
They concluded with the question
What type of man do you admire
I responded . . . Jesus and Houdini
The kid-shrink smiled and turned to my mother
With the following prognosis
It's fortunate you have a child of faith
Churches nowadays have great social service programs
At that, my mother terminated the interview
As we climbed into the car, and I fastened my seatbelt
I could see she was frustrated
When I asked if I did something wrong
She nearly cried and hugged me tight
While telling me . . . I'll find the money somewhere
To get you those magic lessons
I'd rather take my chances with the magician

ANOTHER CASSIDY OPERA

(3)
Battery Park, nobody was around
Until somebody was, a woman alone, holding binoculars
She looked at me—I looked at her and asked
Birds? She nodded yes
She didn't talk – I didn't talk
Instead, she raised those binoculars
And stared everywhere, however . . .
There was nothing to see
I mentioned, in case she hadn't figured it out
There's no birds
She said . . . There will be
And then she said something
Something I found interesting
She said . . . If you examine the fauna
Creatures are creatures
But birds are different
Birds are aliens
They are better than the rest
I didn't disagree

ANOTHER CASSIDY OPERA

(4)

If you discover humanity, you will realize
People are people, but Tom Cassidy, he's an alien
He's better than the rest, if he wanted to, he could be
The wizard behind the curtain
He could write scripts for HBO
Scripts that would ultimately be rejected
For being too clever, void of commercial impact
Once he told me . . . Your set was good
Because you spoke to the crowd as citizens
Instead of consumers
Gosh . . .
Another time he handed me a catalog
For Tannen's Magic on West 34th
Insisting this was the place to be
I went, I saw card tricks
Memorabilia and Houdini's handcuffs
This place was bucket-list material
But this moment, it wasn't perfect
It would have been perfect
Had Cassidy been with me

THE ARBUS SHOW

I thought of New York, how we arrived early
The hotel wouldn't let us check in
You took me uptown to a Madison Avenue gallery
Displaying Diane Arbus photographs
Gallery attendants appeared to be in a lather
In positions suggesting rebuke
My phone rang . . .
A short attendant with long dreadlocks
Gave me the look – You know the look
He rolled his eyes, hissed and sighed
I inched in, placing him in shadow
Before explaining . . . If Arbus was here
She would love me, and we would hate you
Dreadlocks looked frightened, then sad
Then I felt sad and became frightened

ISN'T IT DELICIOUS?

Marilyn, you're dead, but I am alive
Standing on a subway grate
Your subway grate on the southwest corner
Of 52nd and Lexington
There are no signs of any sort
No indications of commemoration
Drip – Drip – Drip, raindrops
Zoom – Zoom, Hustle and Bustle
New York's in motion
While I stand soaked, remembering
The poems you used to write
I loved the one about the bridges
I've read it at gigs
It always gets a big response
Marilyn, you're dead, but I am alive
Issuing a reminder
So you can remember
You are not alone

A HOTEL WHOSE NAME WE WON'T MENTION

(1)
World weary, I laid across the bed
Listening to Yankees radio, we were on the road
At Camden Yards in Baltimore
Getting our asses handed to us by the Orioles
I found little reason to care
The deficit was insurmountable
I began getting tired, my mind drifted
I remembered that O's catcher Matt Wieters
And tried to remember which National League team
Would eventually steal him away
World weary, I fell asleep, only to wake up at 1:20 a.m.
I was half asleep, I was parched
I went in search of Diet A&W root beer
Lights were off, I opened the fridge
It had a burnt-out bulb
So, lights were off
I drank in silence

A HOTEL WHOSE NAME WE WON'T MENTION

(2)
Silence is silent, until it is not
Silence is familiar, until it is not
In darkness I heard a noise
I was half asleep, I heard water rippling
Ever so slightly, in the darkness
I remembered earlier that night
I made a frozen pizza, and upon completion
It was noticed, there was residue
Chunks on the pizza pan
Logic dictated I should soak the pan
So, I filled the sink halfway with water
I was half asleep, I heard water rippling
Perplexed and not a bit amused
I flipped the light switch on
And I couldn't believe it, I wanted to scream
But I was shocked when I witnessed a mouse
Dog paddling across my sink, Jesus help me
Mice on the floor are awful
But a dog paddling sink-mouse
It just doesn't get worse than that

A HOTEL WHOSE NAME WE WON'T MENTION

(3)

In addition to the pizza pan
There was an inverted coffee mug
In the middle of the sink
Paddle mouse headed toward it
Possibly seeking higher ground
Possibly preparing to leap at me
I was half asleep – I was world weary
Now in the darkness, in the almost silence
I had decisions to make, decisions with consequences
I don't like to kill
But I also don't like pestilence and disease
Paddle – Paddle – Paddle
Paddle – Paddle – Paddle
What to do
What to do
I don't like to kill

A HOTEL WHOSE NAME WE WON'T MENTION

(4)

In an act of eventuality, I chose mouse murder
I had limitless options, but I was half asleep
I didn't know how to proceed
Paddle – Paddle – Paddle
Paddle – Paddle – Paddle
The little mouse swam toward the mug
Toward the higher ground
Toward the receptacle I would pick up
And place over the mouse
Sending it to its watery grave
In horror, I listened for mouse screams
I listened for condemnation
From God or some rodent spirit
I heard nothing
I figured the mouse was dead
But then I wondered
Could there be an air pocket under the mug?
Air enough to keep the critter alive
And what if he drowned
Do mice have a different biology?

A HOTEL WHOSE NAME I WON'T MENTION

(5)
If I pulled the carcass from the sink
Would it dry out and attack me
Like the *Fatal Attraction* woman
Or Freddy Krueger
World weary, I made a choice
I would place a heavy weight
On top of the coffee mug
And deal with
Whatever needed to be dealt with
After sunlight entered the kitchen

WOMAN AT THE STRAND

Books – Books and Books
I was holding books
Norman Mailer, Erica Jong, Sylvia Plath
Alex Haley and Peter Benchley
Books – Books and Books
I saw one about how to make cathedral bells
I saw one about learning ventriloquism
I saw one about cannons, I saw one filled
With Edward Hopper paintings
Books – Books and Books
I stood in an aisle next to a woman
Of a certain age who mumbled theories about
Melchizedek, truthfully, I disagreed
With this woman's theology
But she was kind. So, I liked her
When it was apparent it was time to separate
The woman of a certain age said . . . Have a good day
I said . . . I will try
She said . . . There is no need to try
Either you will decide to be happy
Or you won't

KINOKUNIYA BOOKSTORE

We went in because we did
I went in because she did
I had no idea what I was getting into
Books and items, items and books
So many things organized
So many things clean
We went in because we did
I went in because she did
Stumbling into what might be
The biggest selection of origami paper, ever
So many treasures brought back to my hotel
So much time folding cranes
So many cranes, my room looked like the set
Of a low-budget Hitchcock film
Cranes on the windowsill and headboard
Cranes on the desk, soap dispenser and floor
Cranes enough to eventually
Leave housekeeping intrigued
Or disturbed

GIFTS IN BRYANT PARK

Between this and that, I sat at a bench
I had nowhere to go, nothing to do
So, I sat at a bench and stared ahead
There was a public bathroom in front of me
I wasn't looking at it, but it was in my sightline
A man several benches over mentioned . . .
Those are the cleanest bathrooms in New York
I wasn't sure how to process this information
So instead of pondering, I deflected
And pointed to the book in his hands
The man said the book was called . . .
An Attempt at Exhausting a Place in Paris
Written by Georges Perec
The man went on to explain how Perec
Sat in cafés and wrote down everything he saw
And then he wrote different versions
Of these observations, I told the man
That sounds interesting, he said it was
Then he gave it to me for keeps
While reminding me . . .
Those are the cleanest bathrooms in New York

DRUMMER GIRL #1

There she was the drummer girl
Beating down a heater on Bleeker Street
Glaring into oblivion
Was that a look of indifference
I felt shy – I felt fearless
I approached – I confessed
Saw your show last night
You guys were legit
Drummer Girl took a drag
Exhaled and said . . .
The ensemble pitched in
But those were my songs
That was my show
Did you see that crowd, I killed them all
They're all dead now, lying in a pile
Before I could answer, she flicked her cig upward
Into a sky of low-hanging stars
And before that cig hit the ground
She was gone, leaving me to wonder
Why I liked her as much as I did

DRUMMER GIRL #2

Under a flag of some nation other than ours
A familiar face in the presence of an unfamiliar sound
Sweating under a canopy of low-hanging stars
A familiar face, the drummer girl
Beating down a heater, sweating through the fog
To my surprise—She recognized me
To my surprise—She engaged, stating . . .
You were in the club Tuesday
Did you see how I killed that crowd
They're all dead now
I wanted to stay in that moment
I didn't want it to end, but I couldn't find words
Appropriate for contribution
So, I just stood there, sharing her silence
An offering I hope she found pleasant

DRUMMER GIRL #3

I had the impression
That she didn't care that she
Was talking to me
As much as she was talking
She said . . .
Sometimes the stage is covered
With dark patches, dark enough
To make me feel skeptical
But once my eyes become accustomed
I'm able to pick out facial traits
In the audience
Facial traits that report
What I already know
My show – My night
I killed them all
They're dead in a pile

TAXI DRIVER

(1)

I flew into JFK, I've never flown into JFK
Always LaGuardia. No particular reason
But there I was, in JFK, looking for a cab
To take me to the Hilton Garden Inn
A ground transport guy pointed at a cab
At a cabbie half my size and possessed with joy
In the cab, the cabbie said . . .
My name is Hermann, nice to meet you
After introducing myself, I asked . . .
Where did you come from, Hermann said . . .
Indonesia, I asked . . . Jakarta?
Hermann answered enthusiastically
Yes – Yes – Yes, how happy this makes me
You know my home
After a few miles Hermann looked at me
In the rearview mirror
Half my size and possessed with joy
He asked . . . Do you love God
I paused, I smiled, our eyes connected
In the rearview mirror
Yes, Hermann, I love God, Jesus and Mary

TAXI DRIVER

(2)
Zoom – Zoom over bridges, past tightly-knit buildings
We soared, he roared with a righteous indignation
And a miraculous story I was willing to accept
Hermann said . . . Before I came to New York, Danny
I lived in Boston, I drove a limo
They asked me to work a double, I shouldn't have
I was tired, but I needed money for my family
In the middle of the night, I fell asleep at the wheel
In the middle of the highway
God is good Danny, God has angels, God sent angels
And they kicked the undercarriage of the limo
I woke up, I stayed alive, I am thankful
Are you thankful Danny?
It's hard to explain, I was overwhelmed
I trusted Hermann, so I replied . . .
I am thankful, Hermann
Thankful God sent you to me

TAXI DRIVER

(3)
Zoom – Zoom over bridges
Driving closer to skyscrapers, we discussed the Bible
John, Paul and Elijah, when my fare was complete
I asked if he would return 7 a.m. Friday morning
To take me back to JFK
Half my size and possessed with joy, Hermann responded . . .
Yes Danny, you are my brother
Then he shook my hand, and I was happy
Tick – Tock, Friday came to be, on the return trip
We talked about this, we talked about that
Hebrews, Amos and Titus, as we approached the airport
Hermann invited me to come back during a weekend
For BBQ and friendship, since my final departure
Hermann texts me weekly, words of encouragement
And a reminder
We are more than friends
We are brothers

GOTHAM CITY

The marquee outside the Coliseum Bar
Advertised great food and drinks
But once inside, I noticed the tables were empty
Everybody sat at the bar
In a space that didn't require sunshine or enthusiasm
For an hour we drank without talking
While television played the evening news
Halfway through another whiskey soda
The news anchor turned pale as he reported
Adam West, the original Batman, passed away
Everyone became slack-jawed as they journeyed
Through scrambled memories, trying to remember
Their definitive Batman moment
What I wouldn't have given to crawl inside their minds
Then a voice from the shadows asked
If the house was going to buy a round
The bartender bypassed the request
Clicked off the TV and shrugged his shoulders
Before asking
Who's gonna keep our city safe now?

SAINT PATRICK'S CATHEDRAL

The decision was impromptu, it seemed to make sense
Once I crossed the threshold – Once I stepped on holy ground
But then, just like that, something shifted
My spirit altered and I experienced
An immediate suspension of delight
All that space – All those statues
Then the memories, memories of . . .
How the church failed me – How I had failed me
How I had failed the church
I walked past Paul, John and Jesus
But my soul remained anguished
I processed without knowing it, I looked across the Cathedral
I spied a large glass contraption that resembled a penalty box
Containing the image of Mary, hovering
Typically, I'm a back pew guy, but on this day
I went to the front row and dropped to my knees
Hoping the Lord would understand
When things are at their worst, I'm better off
Searching for solace with a woman

KETTLE OF FISH

(1)
When our entourage entered
Everyone surrounding the bar
Fell silent and flashed us a momentary glance
With the understanding, this was their domain
And we'd be allowed to remain without incident
As long as we followed general protocol
The front room was the main assembly
Where fairy lights bounced color
Off bottles, tumblers and mirrors
As ideas and gossip were exchanged
I couldn't help thinking this joint
Was more of a fort than a tavern
The backroom was huge, baby warehouse huge
Absent of light
Filled with high-tech speakers
Blaring
Filled with high-tech speakers
Blaring Tom Petty
"Running Down a Dream"

KETTLE OF FISH

(2)
The entourage set camp in back
But it was hard to hold court
The music was too loud, a new song started
Blaring Tom Petty
"American Girl"
This went on, and on a bit longer
Blaring Tom Petty
"Refugee—Don't Do Me Like That"
"Mary Jane's Last Dance—Yer So Bad"
Strangers in a strange land seldom establish policy
But when a new song started
Blaring Tom Petty
"Free Falling"
Each and every local sang along with the chorus
While one of their vixens crossed into our space
Expressing herself with something between
Interpretive dance and stumble
After a series of hand signals between our crew
The entourage returned to the front room
And commandeered the juke box
After the swipe of a card, Lou Reed came on
Singing "Sweet Jane," the locals hissed

KETTLE OF FISH

(3)
I smiled, asking without malice
I thought New York loved Lou
A self-appointed representative of the locals
Cocked his head and asked . . .
Where are you guys from?
For a brief moment, I studied this advisory
Trying to figure out the level of our conflict
Rookie Mistake – I was drunk
Rookie Mistake – On foreign turf
I wasn't sure how to proceed
So, I told the truth, I'm from Minnesota
After immediate silence, laughter erupted
As a local diplomat explained
That would make you a Vikings supporter
Kettle of Fish happens to be
A Green Bay Packers bar
No shit, I said – No shit, he said
As he went on to explain Aaron Rodgers parties here
Then my new friend bought me a beer
Not knowing I was a cocktail guy
However, this time, I made an exception

EMPIRE PRETTY

She insisted on pastry, muffins or scones
Espresso went without saying
The sun shined romance, making it difficult
For the couple to realize, they were in the midst
Of a future memory that would be cherished
For years to come
The couple walked, passing coffee shops
Boutique bakeries, options and opportunities
He asked . . . Wanna do this, wanna do that
She said no, so the couple walked and walked
And walked beyond that, finally stopping
At the foot of a skyscraper
He said . . . Wanna go up
She said . . . Up or up higher
He said . . . Up – Up
To the highest observation deck
To the 102nd floor, they did, they smiled
Silent, basking, dreaming
Until a man passed by
Looked at her and said to him
Ain't she empire pretty?

NEW YORK CITY PUBLIC LIBRARY

After yogurt and possibly a banana
After experiencing boredom from being alone
I walked and I walked, not knowing where to go
Or what to do, I walked and I walked
Until I saw two big lion statues
I had nowhere to go, nothing to do
So I stopped and stood
Next to one of the two big lion statues
Statues don't talk, so I felt bored and alone
Until two heaven-sent men stood in my vicinity
Guy on the left said to guy on the right
Recently my daughter went to an amusement park
And after buying a cherry snow cone
While she held it in her hand, a bird flew over
And shit directly onto the cherry snow cone
This result made the heaven-sent men laugh
And for the first time in awhile
I began to feel merry

EXODUS AND EXILE

(1)
Somewhere between bagels and the event
We stopped at Mercer Street Books & Records
My companions browsed through vinyl
While I thumbed through a copy of Nabokov's book
Of butterfly illustrations, was it random chance
Or an act of the Holy Ghost, that I found myself
In the religion aisle, staring over piles
Of dusty Bible commentaries
The first one I picked up was Timothy
He never took money for preaching
He built tents with Paul until they had a fight
And went their separate ways
Commentary number two covered the book of Daniel
I smiled because that is my name
I smiled because I knew in Hebrew Daniel meant
God is my judge
Then I remembered many people don't know
That in some ways Daniel is a companion book
To Revelations and end times

EXODUS AND EXILE

(2)
When I was a kid, nuns gave me candy bars
For memorizing . . .
Dare to be a Daniel
Dare to stand alone
Dare to have a purpose firm
And dare to make it known
Next commentary was Exodus
I considered the Hebrews
I considered the phonetics of
Exodus and Exile
I considered exodus occurs after exile
Free and unencumbered, down the aisle
In front of the Jewish religion books
Stood two couples facing each other
They lamented as a young kid circled
While talking to them and himself
Nobody talked to the kid
Occasionally he glanced my way
Free and unencumbered, the two couples
Discussed parenting, in fact the mother
Pointed to the circling kid
Rambling on how he never left his room

EXODUS AND EXILE

(3)

She mentioned phrases like . . .
Hydration and an abundance of canisters
Then she insisted the kid never
Never left his room because . . .
But then she stopped projecting
And I couldn't make out the answer
I grimaced, I furrowed my brow
The kid looked at me and explained
They want me to go outside more
I've been exiled from Play-Doh
I laughed until it occurred to me
I never said "exile" out loud
But that word was becoming popular
Leaving me to wonder
If this was anything more
Than a weird coincidence

ANOTHER ALL-NIGHT CUBAN DINER

(1)

21 hours earlier, the day contained possibilities
I had theories of what that might entail
But at no point did I envision
Sitting soaked at 3 a.m.
In an all-night Cuban diner
Drenched and yawning, I caught a second wind
3 a.m. and this place was buzzing
The energy remained high, conversations serious
A perfect backdrop that reminded me
Of my insignificance, in all the best ways
Momentarily I was separated from the entourage
I wondered if that was predestination
Or simply the result of drunkenness
In the midst of this commotion
I began to feel a calmness which unfortunately
Appears infrequently

ANOTHER ALL-NIGHT CUBAN DINER

(2)

3 a.m. sitting soaked
In an all-night Cuban diner
Where a guy at the next table says in a voice
Loud enough for everyone to hear
I would have killed for those men
I didn't have a father and I wanted their approval
My stomach growled, it was in search of protein
When the server arrived at my table
I pointed at a plate in front of a guy
Sitting at the bar
Silently the server nodded his approval
Before retreating
As I waited, I had an epiphany
And I don't like to use that word
Because it gets overused
But somehow, I became overwhelmed
At the beauty that can only occur
When you are a stranger in a strange land
Eventually I ate my meal
Sobered up and returned to the street
Wondering what was in store for me
On this new day

FLOAT

(1)

I was at that place in Central Park

That place replicated to look like that place in Paris

Where people came to sail model boats

I could tell you it was breathtaking

But truthfully, I didn't give a shit

I was just looking for a place to read my book

As I began to settle in, a young twerp

Was acting spastic while intermittently

Deciding to float his boat

I did my best to ignore him

But the twerp inserted questioning me

Into his routine

The book I was reading was

The Golden Bowl by Fredrick Manfred

A story much like *The Grapes of Wrath* by Steinbeck

Both stories covered poverty during the 1930s

During the Dust Bowl era

Dust Bowl life has always intrigued me

And truthfully, I was starting to believe

Manfred's novel was better than Steinbeck's

In Steinbeck's saga, the Joad family fled

Leaving the Midwest, and they made their way west

To California, to the Promised Land

FLOAT

(2)
Manfred on the other hand flipped the script
In his book, he focused on the Thor family
One of the few families that for better or worse
Was too stubborn to leave
Both of these books are great reads
But Manfred is simply a better writer
The twerp ate ice cream, the twerp drank soda
The twerp handed me his remote control
Urging me to cast off, I was reluctant
He was persistent
Zoom – Zoom how relaxing
Zoom – Zoom feel the glide
Just when I considered issuing a compliment
The twerp asked . . .
If I could sail anywhere in the world
Where would I go, I thought about it
I answered . . . I'd go to Russia
The Odessa Steps, maybe the Siberian Arctic
To which the twerp replied . . .
That's stupid, if you get to go anywhere
It's best to go someplace that has a volcano
After thinking about it
I didn't disagree

CONEY ISLAND – KINDA

(1)

You wanted to go . . . me, indifferent
Lots of time on the subway
When there was so much to see
In the Village, in Hell's Kitchen
Tribeca as well
You wanted to go . . . me, indifferent
But just like most times
If my world is to remain happy
Boy follows Girl
Subway was packed, until it wasn't
Across the aisle, two teenage girls
The one with braids, Blah-Blah-Blah
The one sporting a pixie didn't say a word
Braids shifted topics every minute
If you judged her by her conversation
You'd probably be left wanting
But in the flesh, that was a deal breaker
Her features were interesting
Shelly Duvall exotic
You tuned out and read Paula Hawkins
Her second book which you claimed
Was only half as good as her first

CONEY ISLAND – KINDA

(2)

I pulled out *The White Album*
By Joan Didion, recently I finished her book
Let Me Tell You What I Mean
The essay about Nancy Reagan—Priceless
These essays were my baptism
Into the world of essays
I honestly believed Didion
Was some kind of messiah
But what was it, nine weeks later
I got turned on to Eve Babitz
Gosh . . . she blew Didion out of the water
Nine weeks after that
I started reading essays by men
Johnathan Franzen and a few other yahoos
I'm not an expert, but I have an opinion
In the essay camp, guys should step back
It's a world dominated by women
I don't remember what page I was on
But I remember you looked up
And out the window
Before squinting and whispering . . .
Shit, we had overshot our stop
By a beyond stupid distance

CONEY ISLAND – KINDA

(3)
After putting the books away
You volunteered to navigate us
Back to the stop we departed from
I sat quiet, watching Braids and Pixie
Blah-Blah-Blah, Blah Blah
Then a thing happened
I remember thinking, the next few minutes
Might determine if our day could be salvaged
Blah-Blah-Blah, Braids didn't miss a beat
And my needle started tilting toward frustration
Until Braids said to Pixie . . .
That's why your dad wins
He kills everyone with a deadly friendliness
"Deadly Friendliness," I thought
I love the sound of that
One day I'll work it into a poem

ALONE WITH MONET

After paying the suggested donation
It was as if a magnetic force pulled me to the second floor
To a space in the presence of Claude Monet's lily pads
I heard buzzing conversations in dialects I couldn't decipher
Except I knew the tone was reverent
15 minutes later, the mob around me began to thin out
And I was alone in front of the painting
Now my entire body was consumed by joy, head to toe
Until a woman in a T-shirt
Indicating she may have run a 10K in Oakland
Sidled up to me and asked
If traveling to Monet's Garden would be the ultimate vacation
I told her I would prefer to stay in New York with the painting
Because if you visited the beautiful gardens in France
People would strike up conversations
And that would ruin the moment

OH MARY

(1)
They said it was hilarious
A play about Mary Todd Lincoln
Her character was played by a dude
Lincoln was queer
John Wilkes Booth was his lover
It was getting rave reviews
I said OK, I went on my way
Down Christopher Street
Toward the Lucille Lortel Theatre
Lots of people were out
But the mass was calm
Lots of people were out
Nobody seemed to desire attention
Down the way I spied a short woman
With a tall man, the woman was making noise
As I came within earshot, I tried to determine
If this voice was jovial or angry
It turned out to be the latter

OH MARY

(2)
As my route became even with their space
Mercy was not employed
If anything, the woman ramped up, saying . . .
He's your child too, think of that
Think about how the outcome not only relies
On the decisions you make
But it also relies on the ones you don't
And I'm beginning to notice
You aren't capable of deciding anything
The guy shuffled forward
Explaining to her, while looking at me
And saying . . . When I consider our son
It's not my wisdom I consider
I seek God's and from my experience
It usually takes God ten minutes
To deliver an answer
A prudent person will invest ten minutes
The woman stepped back flummoxed
I was beyond intrigued
I wanted to know how things played out
But my pace refused to falter
And I continued on my way

WEST VILLAGE JAZZ CRAWL

(1)
Cat's name was Gordo, an older guy
A former club owner in Harlem who couldn't make a go of it
After his tipping point followed its natural course
He shuttered the club and started a side hustle
Renting himself out as a jazz tour guide
We discussed be bop, we discussed horns
He strolled me by the courthouse where Billie Holiday
Got the book thrown at her
Gordo told me this – Gordo told me that
I mentioned remembering something I read
From Bob Dylan's book *Chronicles*
Where he mentioned coming to the Village
And hanging with Tiny Tim
What an unlikely pair, commented Gordo
They played for free, or sometimes for hamburgers
Then Gordo stopped on the sidewalk
And scrolled on his phone, after a moment
About the length of time it took my mother to snap
Our family Christmas picture, Gordo said . . .
Ta da, here it is, here's the picture of me and Tiny Tim
This was decades ago, I was part of a group
That walked across America, protesting nuclear energy
Somewhere in Ohio

WEST VILLAGE JAZZ CRAWL

(2)

We ran into Tiny Tim and that made us happy
Until he found out our mission and became disappointed
Because he believed nuclear energy was the next big thing
After Cellar Dogs, but before Mona's
We stopped at Arthur's Tavern and sat at a reserved table
Where we ordered cocktails and discussed Horace Silver
Blah – Blah – Blah, eventually the topic became exhausted
So, Gordo took this opportunity to hit the head
Before the band took the stage
I sat alone, I sat listening to a couple next to me
Discussing their disdain for their children
Who had created a rendezvous point
Where they would meet in the event of a zombie attack
The plan sounded extensive, but the parents didn't get an invite
And they were pissed, Gordo returned, the band came out
They looked like kids, they probably were
Their outfits were nothing special
Something off the rack – Something from TJ Maxx
They gathered their instruments
While flashing monotone expressions

WEST VILLAGE JAZZ CRAWL

(3)

3-2-1 . . . BOOM, the set started
Technically they were perfect, technology was employed
They used phones and iPads, technically they were perfect
Gordo melted into the jam, it was wonderful seeing him
Happy in his element, after the first set he asked my opinion
I mentioned it was good, they were good, but they had no soul
Gordo paused and processed before reminding me
Today's kids are a different sunrise, but I'm just thankful
That the sun still exists
When the night was over, when morning crawled
I stood in the street with Gordo, who confessed . . .
It's hard at my age to find friends who will hit the clubs
On Tuesday night, or any night for that matter
So, I want to leave you with my thanks
And then he gave me one of those guy hugs
A half hug, a form of contact that makes me feel awkward
But for reasons unknown to me
On this particular occasion
The sentiment was appreciated

A NIGHT AT THE WHITE HORSE TAVERN

(1)
After the rain – Before the show
Ken approached Jen
Took her drink order and offered when
Dylan Thomas set his personal best
It was 16 doubles of Jack Daniels
A total that toppled, so much so
Dylan Thomas slumped – Two days later
Dylan Thomas thumped – Two days later
Onto the floor of the bar at the Chelsea Hotel
POOF – Just like that Dylan was dead
I asked Ken, tell me when
And maybe I will try for 17
To which he responded . . .
If you're shooting for the record
I'm on all night

A NIGHT AT THE WHITE HORSE TAVERN

(2)
After the rain – Before the show
I leaned sideways, pointing at them
Two women slurring playfully
Mumbling through a narrative
Tangled in a cocktail fog
The woman on the right
Explained to the woman on the left
When you're on a train
Passing through hell
Never get off, because if you do
You'll remain in hell, forever
Then they became silent
Neither one spoke until
The woman on the left deduced
If you stay on that hell train
If you stay on long enough
Eventually you'll be able to get off
In Texas

BILLY DON'T LOSE MY NUMBER

(1)
I don't have many friends, people think I do
I don't, I have acquaintances
A large collection of acquaintances
But Billy is my friend
Montgomery, Alabama
Asheville, North Carolina
Now New York City
Billy has been the common denominator
On my book tours
We discussed meeting at the Hotel Chelsea
We mentioned afternoon
Without pinpointing a time
Clip – Clop, passing time
Clip – Clop, pounding pavement
Then . . . when I found myself unsure
Of which way I was tilting
I found myself at the end of a blur
I found myself in the lobby

BILLY DON'T LOSE MY NUMBER

(2)
Many people have their favorite version
Of who or what they identify the Chelsea with
I choose Sid Vicious, a hero of my youth
But if your choice is different
I won't begrudge you
I find myself in the lobby, I don't spy Billy
So, I sit on a loveseat that considers itself chic
I don't spy Billy, so I consider
My youth, the musicians, punk rock
Why does it make me smile when I consider
Every living Sex Pistol is currently on Medicare
Tick – Tock, time passes
Tick – Tock, the building is quiet
There's something about the energy
Or lack of it, in this building
I don't like it, and that makes me sad
On my phone I see a story
The National Guard is joining
An increased NYC police force
To canvass the subways
With hopes of providing protection

BILLY DON'T LOSE MY NUMBER

(3)
Billy is on the subway, or supposed to be
And now I begin to worry about him
Not like a mother
But like a friend, an old man friend
Old enough to consider
The world is becoming meaner
Or indifferent
I don't like these things in my world
Or in my head
So I break camp and wander aimlessly
Clip – Clop, passing time
Clip – Clop, pounding pavement
Alone in New York
Only for a moment
Alone in New York
Throughout day and into night
So tired – stretched out on my bed
So tired – with an aching body
Aching as a body will
In well-written NYC essays

BILLY DON'T LOSE MY NUMBER

(4)

I rub my legs – I rub my eyes

I rub my legs until my phone alerts me

Billy sent a text

He mentions family

He mentions Spike Lee film sets

He mentions cocktails

Like the one he is having

At the bar in the Chelsea

He mentions he likes that the staff continues

Calling him Sir

Even though he doesn't consider himself

A Sir

This makes me smile

This makes me feel better

My eyes start closing, I'm falling asleep

But before I do, I realize

Tomorrow is going to be swell

WOMAN IN A BREAD AISLE

(1)
Dateline: Whole Foods, Bryant Park
I was looking for crackers, which was close to bread
And in that bread aisle stood a beautiful woman
Her hair was white, she had high cheekbones
She wore a babushka and spoke
With traces of a Euro accent
She was looking at loaves
While holding a multigrain boule
I sidled up and said . . . I prefer sourdough
She said . . . I want rye
But what they call rye, I call shit
I should have asked her where she was from
But I didn't, our conversation started
With discussing rye percentages
Brioche sponges and sweetening agents
Next the woman segued to the Saints
When I told her how much I adored
Saint Faustina, she lit up and asked
Where I went to church
I mentioned I didn't, I mentioned I missed it
I mentioned I didn't believe the doctrine anymore

WOMAN IN A BREAD AISLE

(2)
The babushka woman smiled
While assuring me in tone and comfort
You don't have to believe
But it's still important to practice your faith
I didn't know what to say
I didn't know how to proceed
So, I shifted gears and changed the narrative
To crackers
After we said our goodbyes and separated
It occurred to me this woman was genius because
Just because you don't believe, that doesn't mean
There isn't something worth believing in

LADY LIBERTY AND THE SCOTTISH

(1)
Mount Rushmore – Check
Liberty Bell – Check
Grand Canyon, Watergate and Alcatraz
Check, Check and Check
Next up, Ellis Island
Next up, that big feminine statue
Given to us by the French
I bought tickets, or maybe she did
Either way we headed to the place
Where you catch the ferry
At the place where you board
The gathering space seems as if
It is designed to collect cattle or sardines
In the midst of this scrum
Even though it was morning
People didn't smell good
A funk seemed to hover
I began to feel lightheaded

LADY LIBERTY AND THE SCOTTISH

(2)
As people continued packing in tighter
I became claustrophobic
Anxiety began kicking my shins
I began to chant
I employed Jedi mind tricks
As things began to settle
I began feeling a level of calm
Nobody goes to the Statue of Liberty alone
People travel in groups
Most groups have an alpha who takes control
Whether their travel companions like it or not
A guy standing to my right pointed to our left and said . . .
The woman in yellow and black
She and her friends, God they are loud
Don't they sound like motion-sensor witches
I loved that line, but I soon forgot it
The thing that stuck in my mind
Was the guy standing on my right
Was wearing a Scottish polo

LADY LIBERTY AND THE SCOTTISH

(3)
As we boarded the ferry, people spread out
On the water, our groups combined energy
Seemed quiet, almost reverent
I was standing, or sitting, I don't remember
What I do remember is
It occurred to me for the first time
That Scotland had two flags
Flag #1 –
It's dark blue with a huge white X
It's an honest flag, a noble flag
A flag for those who smirk instead of smiling
Flag #2 –
It's yellow and regal, with a big red lion on it
To be honest
I'm not sure I like this version so much

LADY LIBERTY AND THE SCOTTISH

(4)
I could have asked the guy to the right
How and why
Scotland has two different flags
He probably would have known
But then I figured I'd look it up
When I got back home
But I never did
I forgot Scotland had two flags
And haven't looked it up since
Truthfully, it's probably not
The kind of thing you need to know
But I do want to know
Why does Scotland have two flags?

TRIBECA CAFÉ

(1)

Satan and sunshine
Blue bloods and red wine
Gathered at a place with limited seating
I asked them if we could join them at their table
A woman named Margo, their party's alpha
Welcomed us aboard
Sweat stains were visible
On predictable parts of her blouse
Cocktails and appetizers
Cocktails and conversations
Is it just me, or do conversations in August
Always seem just a bit drawn out
Satan and moonshine
Sots drinking red wine
Gathered in a place otherwise empty
I asked Margo to join us
One final drink, one final story
Her voice slurred, her eyes buckled
As she explained coming of age
In the Midwest . . .

TRIBECA CAFÉ

(2)
It was senior prom, we had a party
Cases of wine, cases of beer
Were made available
And we drank to a point
Where nothing seemed sensible
Margo continued . . .
In the darkest part of morning
Before the sun comes up
My sister and I drank shots
In the back of a pickup
Which would eventually flip
Throwing us deep into a cornfield
People died, I was lucky
Broken arm, cut-up face
I laid in the cornfield for hours
I laid in the cornfield till sunrise
When I saw my father
Who gave me half a glance
Stepped over me and asked . . .
Where's your sister?

WOMAN IN A PONCHO

(1)
In Central Park, at Shakespeare in the Park
A woman in a poncho recalled Battery Park
And it's one-time famed celebrity, Zelda
Not Fitzgerald, Zelda the turkey
A long-time resident who ruled the roost
For close to a decade
Underneath the poncho, the woman in the poncho
Placed her hands in her back pockets
Bette Davis style, as she spoke with a man
Who appeared to be enamored
As I listened to the woman in a poncho
My mind began to drift
My mind began to consider
Being beautiful in a poncho
In Central Park, at Shakespeare in the Park
Was legit
The enamored guy
Seemed to grab for conversational threads
That would allow him to stay in the presence
Of the woman in the poncho

WOMAN IN A PONCHO

(2)
I had the feeling the woman in the poncho
Realized her power and relished the attention
At one point she asked the enamored man . . .
Do you know where turkeys sleep
The enamored man returned a glance
That indicated he might be stepping
Into a trick question
So, the lady in a poncho repeated
Do you know where turkeys sleep
The enamored man shook his head no
To the delight of the woman in the poncho
Who informed those present . . .
They sleep in trees
The enamored man insisted not
The woman in a poncho smiled
While countering with
They sleep in trees, 35 feet high
As an eavesdropper I was uncertain
What game the lady in the poncho was playing
Why was she trying to sell such silliness

WOMAN IN A PONCHO

(3)

As my mind did its best to sort out these details
The enamored man called . . . Bullshit!
To which the woman in the poncho responded
They do, they do sleep up in the trees
35 feet high, if you don't believe me
Google it
The enamored man took her word for it
But I didn't, I wanted to know the truth
I had no reason to build bonds
With the woman in a poncho
So, I Googled . . .
Do turkeys sleep in trees
As the answer was revealed
I thought to myself
Well now, I'll be horsewhipped

THE BOX

(1)
At the corner, about to cross
At the corner, my head swiveled
Looking across the street, catty – corner
There sat a man on an inverted bucket
Holding a metallic box
It wasn't a store-bought one
It looked like the type of box
A proficient metal worker would construct
The man didn't fidget, he sat erect
Maintaining a posture that seemed to prioritize
The safety of the box
On the corner, standing next to me
Some random kid, 20 . . . maybe 22
He was wearing a Phillies baseball cap
I asked him if he was from Philly
He nodded no
I asked why he was wearing a Phillies cap
The kid shrugged his shoulders
And when I noticed his empty palms
Were aimed toward the sky
I wondered if that was intentional

THE BOX

(2)
Shifting gears, I asked the kid not from Philly
What's up with the guy across the street
What's up with that box
The kid not from Philly said
This wasn't the first time he'd seen the guy
Or the box, but he didn't know
What was in the box
But one day when the sun was shining
The box blasted reflections of brightness
That pissed off traffic to the point
They started honking and swearing
But the man on a bucket
The man with a box, didn't budge
He just sat motionless
I pointed out to the kid not from Philly
That the box looked like it had purpose
Like transporting bombs
The kid informed me bomb boxes are smaller
To which I replied . . . You're fucking with me
How would you know that?
The kid didn't answer

THE BOX

(3)
One minute, seven minutes
Twelve minutes passed
The man with the box didn't move
I didn't move
The kid not from Philly remained motionless
Finally, I asked the kid . . .
Go ask the guy what's in the box
The kid just shook his head, no
To which I responded . . .
There's $20 in it for you
All you have to do is ask
The kid not from Philly looked at me
Like I was stupid, before asking . . .
Have you ever heard of Risk versus Reward
And with that, he stepped back
And slid out of the moment

STRAWBERRY FIELDS

(1)
If I had to pick a day over the course of my life
Where I held my highest trajectory
Physically, economically and spiritually
It was that day we stumbled upon hippies and tourists
But mostly hippies, across the street
From the Dakota in Central Park
I probably would have walked past
I don't wear jeans or bandanas
I probably would have walked past
I don't call guys "Man"
I call them "Sir"
But she sat down with a group of dusty people
And sang along as Fuzz Face played
"Rocky Raccoon" on an acoustic guitar
One song led to another, and . . .
To my horror, I sensed in my companion's posture
She was settling in
Everybody shared the music
Everybody shared delight

STRAWBERRY FIELDS

(2)

If I had to pick a day over the course of my life
Where I held my highest trajectory
It was this day, but . . . these hippies
I couldn't buy into their . . .
Politics
Wardrobes
Vernacular
They smiled, just because
Using phrases like . . .
Peace
Far Out
Groovy
I wanted to go, but knew I couldn't
They were all singing
"We All Live in a Yellow Submarine"
I tried to act genuine
I tried to act like I cared
But I didn't

STRAWBERRY FIELDS

(3)
I tried to be tolerant
But some teenage boy standing next to me
Stood next to his mother
They wore matching feather earrings
They giggled, they smiled
They sang and they sang
And they sang until they didn't
And that's the moment my life took a turn
Feather-Boy said to Feather-Mom
John is my favorite Beatle
I like his solo albums most
George is pretty good too
Feather-Mom didn't respond with words
She just smiled and seemed to be happy
I remember telling myself not to do it
But I did, I used words, I voiced my opinion
Paul is by far the best Beatle
Jesus, haven't you listened to Paul's "Ram" album?

STRAWBERRY FIELDS

(4)
Feather-Boy didn't respond
He just flashed a puzzled look
Toward Feather-Mom
Who flashed a look of disappointment
At me, then they departed without speaking
When they were out of sight
I felt relief and did my best
To forget my thoughtless blunder
But a guy sitting on a bench
A guy who looked like Christopher Walken
Deer Hunter Walken
Put me back on the hook
When he said . . .
They were happy, but you ruined that
Because you had to be right
Was it worth wrecking a moment?

STRAWBERRY FIELDS

(5)

I felt pretty awful
A bit defensive too
I considered returning an answer
That would have put *Deer Hunter* Walken
In his place, but I thought about it
He was right
And eventually I fessed up
And apologized
To which *Deer Hunter* Walken
Responded with a message
Delivered in a tone of forgiveness . . .
All's good, self-awareness takes time
Don't feel bad about it
I've probably had a little bit more experience
After all, I am a poet

WE TALKED ABOUT NEW YORK

(1)
The commission stated
I had six months to compile
No fewer than 15
No more than 20
Questions to ask Isabella Rossellini
At the fireside conversation
The discourse was to run
A minimum of 40 minutes
But . . .
Not to exceed 45

WE TALKED ABOUT NEW YORK

(2)
On the evening of the event
I entered the venue
The space was quiet
Caterers and security
Went about their business
On the stage were two chairs
Side by side
At a closeness that denoted
Intimacy

WE TALKED ABOUT NEW YORK

(3)
As the mob filed in
I watched from the shadows
As they ate and drank
It occurred to me
Every event that ever was
Are all the same
If you watch from the rafters
You can't help but notice
Beautiful people
Tend to get eclipsed
By louts

WE TALKED ABOUT NEW YORK

(4)
Summoned by security
I reported to the Green Room
With the understanding
I was to give Isabella
A synopsis
Of our upcoming
Fireside conversation

WE TALKED ABOUT NEW YORK

(5)
As I stood
She sat clutching
An Italian Greyhound
As I stood
She never mentioned herself
She never mentioned our show
Instead, she said with an accent
I won't try to replicate
Good evening Mr. Klecko
What shall we discuss
Your poems
Or your sourdough starter?

WE TALKED ABOUT NEW YORK

(6)
Once we took the stage
The lights were so bright
I couldn't see the audience
The lights were so bright
I heard 1000 voices
Connected to people I couldn't see
The lights were so bright
But off to my right
Sat Isabella
She looked happy
She looked calm
The thought occurred to me
We were in this together
And once I realized this
I felt invincible

WE TALKED ABOUT NEW YORK

(7)
We could have talked about escapades
Anywhere in Europe
But for whatever reason
On this particular night
Isabella talked about New York
Manhattan
And the apartment of her childhood
It remained fairly empty
Empty enough to serve as a racetrack
For herself and a tricycle
That repeated laps constantly
We talked about New York
Chickens
Family
And love

WE TALKED ABOUT NEW YORK

(8)
We also talked about Russell
A pet raccoon kept by Marlon Brando
In his small apartment off Broadway
We discussed *Casablanca*
And childhood kangaroos
We discussed lots of things
Most of which
Pertained to Isabella's activism
And commitment to animals
But my favorite part of the evening
Was question number 15
When I asked . . .

WE TALKED ABOUT NEW YORK

(9)
My mother is 83, she lives with cats
She mentioned to me recently
That the older she gets
The better she understands
The silence that she shares
With her cats

WE TALKED ABOUT NEW YORK

(10)
That's when I reminded Isabella
You're the one
With a master's degree in animal behavior
Then I asked if my mom was on to something
Can silence be used to strengthen
Our relationship with our pets
Isabella paused and pondered
Before replying . . .

WE TALKED ABOUT NEW YORK

(11)
Your mother is wise
I haven't thought of this
With my animals I seldom consider silence
But I do spend a great deal of time
Trying to keep them away from noise
Then she stopped talking
And stared at me and smiled
For a brief moment
I felt as if we were alone
I felt safe
I felt happy
Gosh
I wish my mother could have been there

THE END

Closing Thoughts on Isabella Rossellini

By Julie Pfitzinger

Klecko asked me to add a coda to *We Talked About New York* by sharing my thoughts on Isabella Rossellini. I had the privilege of serving as her "minder" at the event you just read about.

I could fill pages with musings on this kind and gracious woman who is an international superstar but exudes such a down-to-earth charm. I was waiting at the back door of the event center, along with two security professionals, when her car pulled up and I watched her walk across a Minneapolis parking lot in a brilliant teal and purple Pucci – flowing pants and top. An elegant woman with a face that was at once familiar and a stunning surprise. And as we started walking and chatting, my nerves slowly calmed.

Klecko has written eloquently about that night, so I'll tell you about two experiences I had that he didn't see. After dinner, I escorted Isabella up to a restroom that had been reserved for her exclusive use. As much as I wanted to go in and watch her re-apply her lipstick – the closest I'd ever get to a behind-the-scenes Vogue photo shoot – I refrained, but that didn't stop me from asking her about her lip color as we made our way back downstairs to the party.

"Lancôme made it just for me, it is called 'Mademoiselle Isabella,'" she explained. "At first I thought it was too blue, but I like it now." (Note to her Instagram followers: she wears that shade often and mentions it frequently. Note to anyone interested: I ordered a tube of 'Mademoiselle Isabella' for myself the very next day. I wear it often.)

After I accompanied her back to the parking lot at the end of the evening, where she disappeared into the night, I returned to the makeshift Green Room to collect my things. There on the table sat the small lint roller that someone had hurriedly procured for Isabella after she spent several minutes holding that Italian Greyhound whose big strands of hair landed on her (likely expensive) black cardigan.

Without hesitation, I picked up the lint roller, slipped it into my bag, and went to find Klecko to compare notes about a magical evening.

KLECKO NATION

In the past I have been known to include
Value-added installments
After the conclusion of my book
I would like to continue this tradition
By including an essay written about a trip
To New York City twenty years ago
By a friend of mine
Who read it to me last year
Over the phone
While I was touring *A Bakeable Feast*
Last April across Times Square
The piece is called *Babel*
Its author is Erica Christ
She has run a small non-profit
Theater company for several decades
While paying her bills working as
A beer maiden in her family's German beer hall
In Minneapolis
I really like this piece
And hope you will as well

Babel

By Erica Christ

On a trip to New York City a few years ago, I distinctly remember sitting on the airplane as it descended and dreading the trip. I had impulsively decided to go hear a friend's play reading. I couldn't really afford the trip; I had a hard time finding a decent hotel room; I wasn't going to get to actually see my friend for more than a couple of hours. As the plane descended, I was asking myself, why did I think this was a good idea? And, as though in a regular conversation, I answered myself: there is something here for you. It was so clear, so direct. The plane landed and I emerged into the airport with my eyes wide open.

As a rule I don't hear voices. But at the time I was reading Carl Jung's *Memories, Dreams, Reflections* so I felt I ought to heed this call in case it was from my unconscious. And, as mysterious messages go, I rather liked the sound of this one: there is something here for you.

Part of the reason hotel rooms were so scarce was that artists Christo and Jean-Claude had filled Central Park with orange fabric gates lining many of the walkways. People were coming from all over the world to see it. Actually, as near as I could tell, people were coming from all over the world to stand in Central Park and talk on their cell phones. I did go through the formality of asking myself if I thought The Gates was the thing that was here for me. I thought no.

It was quite a bit more interesting and impressive than I thought it would be. Pictures don't do it justice. What was interesting was the experience of moving around the park and seeing these long orange lines and curves coming in and out of view. The height and width of the gates are such that you really did get the sense of making an entrance over and over again. It was an unusually warm February day so I stayed in the park and found a place to read.

The play reading was in, guess what, a basement. I knew the play and liked it quite a bit, so I enjoyed the reading, more or less. We went to a decent but not terribly interesting bar after the reading and I did my best not to embarrass my friend in front of the people who were considering producing her play. It was, in the literal sense, what I had come to New York City for, but I had no doubt that it was not the thing that was here for me.

I was not at this point impatient to find the thing that was here for me. I had actually enjoyed my day and I had two more before I left for home. I briefly considered the possibility that the thing that was here for me was simply the distraction of being somewhere else and clearing my mind of mental clutter that usually plagues me and that caused me to regret this trip before I had even arrived. I decided if this search was in any way a figment of my own unruly mind, it is not to be something so tidy, so cute.

The hotel I stayed at was in the 90s on the west side. It was an area that I had not explored before so after breakfast on my second day I started ambling around. One thing I always look for in New York is accoutrement for my hair. If anyone in the Midwest has long hair, they must only put it in a pony-tail because you can't find any good clips, pins or combs anywhere. Not only can you usually find stuff for long hair in regular drug stores in New York, but wholesale beauty shops are all over the place and not picky about whether or not their customers actually have their own salons.

I wandered toward the park and back out again. Before I knew it, I was nearing Times Square. I walked by the place where the play reading had been. I got a cup of tea at Starbucks. I decided to try to find some matzo ball soup for lunch. I ended up in the garment district which was moderately interesting, I didn't know where I was going, really. I was very alert because I was still trying to find this thing that was here for me but wasn't very directed, I ended up near

Chinatown and, even though I knew I would get lost and I was hungry, I decided to plunge in.

Chinatown erupts around me. Cymbals and drums and confetti are all around me. Dragons dance up and down sidewalks and in and out of businesses. It's Chinese New Year. Acrobatic kids are performing in the centers of circles of people. Firecrackers are going off. Near the heart of Chinatown, where the streets bend just so, the sounds of the celebrations bounce off the walls of the buildings and amplify and repeat. Among the crowd of people are parents pointing to the dragons and drummers so their children don't miss anything; couples adorned with colored streamers and confetti; older people watching from low stools outside shops; sharp looking men in suits who disappear in and out of doorways. I love the exuberance of this celebration; and I love that I don't have any idea what the signs say, what the symbols mean, what comes next in the old ritual. I love that moments before I was in a world whose signs I could read, near people whose language I speak and suddenly I am transported away.

This is it, I thought. This is what's here for me. I felt so happy, which is unusual for me. I couldn't figure out why this was the thing that was here for me, but I figured I ought to quit while I was ahead.

I walked down to Katz's but it was a total zoo so I got a lox sandwich from Russ and Daughters and looked for a place to sit down on a bench and eat. I had not yet seen Ground Zero so I headed in that direction. I ate as I walked. My legs hurt. And I was getting blisters on my feet. But I wasn't far from Ground Zero so I kept going.

Ground Zero was a whole different thing seeing it for myself. It may be that the pictures can do no more than document in some cases. Or it may be that one's vision is simply taken over by imagination in some cases so one isn't just seeing, but also feeling and projecting.

At the time I was there, there was still a lot of garbage at the site. So I watched people in little bobcat machines push the garbage around. The surrounding buildings still had scaffold and supports up

111

around them. I was surprised that very little commercialization had sprung up. Nothing for sale. No hawking or soliciting. Very few signs. It was, at least at that time, allowed to just exist, naked and silent, to represent itself without interpretation or translation. I do believe, though, that if you didn't know what had happened there, you would still smell something. You wouldn't need signs or displays to tell you that something terrible had happened there, that you were looking at a big, open wound.

I had a hard time tearing myself away, though I wasn't looking for anything in particular and didn't even know what to think, really. It occurred to me that this might be what was here for me. This is a piece in the puzzle of life here now.

My brains were a little bit scrambled at this point so when I decided to walk down to and across the Brooklyn Bridge I actually thought that was a good idea. My legs were almost numb. But I forgot all about my legs when the span of the bridge came into view. The beauty of the lines and shapes against the sky was so calming, so meditative. Maybe this is it, I thought, this geometric fun house. This is what's here for me.

I got partway across the bridge and turned around. I had walked from 94th Street all the way to the Brooklyn Bridge, and not directly either. I was afraid I had actually injured my legs. I gingerly stepped down into the subway station and rode the train all the way back to the hotel.

It snowed overnight, I had slept well but my legs were still killing me. I staggered through the slush to the nearest drug store so I could have some acetaminophen for breakfast.

Then I went back to the park and saw the Gates in the snow. It was like a whole different park, a whole different installation. The orange fabric looked like it was desperately trying to send a message. Look here! This way! Follow me! Watch out! I liked the alarming effect.

I should have learned my lesson but didn't and I walked down to the Natural History Museum. Once there I had to sit down in almost every room I visited because my legs hurt so much. Going into the museum I felt sure that there was something in there for me. I'm kind of a natural history buff and have a high tolerance for exhibit notes, side bars, explanatory signs and interactive displays. I also like fossils, rocks, bones and dioramas, I was sure I was going to at least enjoy my visit and probably find the thing, the real thing that was here for me.

Sadly, I was distracted by how much my legs hurt. I wasn't paying close attention as I should have been so I got turned around and kept going into the same rooms over and over again. If there was something in there for me, I completely failed to find it. I bought a souvenir coffee mug and left, defeated.

I had some acetaminophen for lunch and found a place to sit and read for the afternoon. Jung is challenging to read; tracking the exploration of language of the unconscious requires focus and surrender that I can't always muster. It was extra challenging for me to read while New York City swirled and swelled around me. There is a chance though, I thought, that the thing that is here for me is in the book that I brought with me. I would have been very annoyed if that had been the case but the sly humor of it wouldn't have escaped me. No matter how little you understand of another language (even the language of the unconscious), you understand when a joke has been made at your expense.

Under the circumstances I decided to spend the money on a taxi to take me to dinner. I went to an Indian restaurant which I had been to on previous visits. I don't get many chances to eat out alone anymore so I was looking forward to it. I had a nice meal. I chatted a little bit with the people at the table next to me. I read a little bit of my book. I met my friend for a drink later on and then turned in. The evening was entirely uneventful and there was no sign of anything that was here for me.

I always leave New York City with a little bit of relief. I always enjoy my visits and there is never enough time to do the things and go to the places that I want to. But it drains me. It may be true that whether or not I know it, I am always looking for something when I'm there and the search is exhausting.

Sitting on the plane I thought about my trip. I wondered if I had found the thing that was there for me. Yes, yes I had. But no more about it came to mind. Not which thing it was, not what it meant or why I needed it.

I had an in-flight snack of acetaminophen and pulled out a magazine. I was hoping for something moderately interesting but easily digestible. I was hoping to relax with something that was in my own language, without riddles and puzzles.

After ten minutes I went back to my book. I preferred the challenge of it. There's no going back to the world before Babel. There's nothing there for me anyway.

KLECKO NATION

Years before Julie Pfitzinger became my publisher
She was my editor at Saint Paul Magazine
For close to two decades, I have watched Julie
Travel in entourages and alone
Attending fresh Broadway plays
Or attending art openings
It is because of her, I have come to believe
You don't have to live in New York City
To have a Big Apple attitude
Submitted for your approval
Is an essay
I'm pretty sure after you read it
You'll see why I like her style

In the Midst

By Julie Pfitzinger

I'm standing in the middle of a lively cocktail party. All around me, men and women dressed in the fashion of the 1960s, are chatting in low tones, moving slowly, standing in duos or trios, raising glasses to their lips, smiling, nodding, greeting someone on their left, on their right.

I'm not actually at this party. I'm in a gallery at MoMA in June 2022. This installation is called "Marta Minujín's MINUCODE." She's an Argentine artist, still prolific at 81, who was commissioned in 1968 to create this work for The Center for Inter-American Relations in New York City.

Minujín hosted four cocktail parties with guests who worked in the arts, business, fashion and politics. The parties were filmed and melded together for MINUCODE. At its completion, she invited the participants to return to see the final work.

At the time, Minujín said, "I wanted them to see themselves 'backward,' to observe their own behaviors, to watch their own social interactions."

For me, right now, there are no social interactions. I am not only alone in this gallery, but I am also alone in New York City.

It's my second trip here in just three months – for me, that's very unusual. Earlier in the year, deciding to grab a bucket list opportunity, I bought a ticket to see an April performance of *Plaza Suite* with Sarah Jessica Parker and Matthew Broderick at the Hudson Theatre. A spring trip from St. Paul to NYC sounded ideal.

As it turned out, COVID wasn't entirely finished with disrupting life. The day before the performance, while already in New York, I received an email that both actors had contracted COVID and the show I was scheduled to see was cancelled. I was offered the opportunity to attend a performance in June or receive a full refund.

Obviously for me, this rescheduled ticket required more than a subway ride. As I stood in the alley next to the Richard Rodgers Theatre waiting for the doors to open to see my last minute "second choice" matinee, *Hamilton*, (which was amazing, naturally), a friend called me on my cell. I relayed the story of the cancelled show, lamented COVID, spoke of my disappointment and mentioned the complicated offer of a June ticket.

"Why wouldn't you go?" my friend asked. "Of course you will. Why wouldn't you?"

So I did.

It was the morning of the *Plaza Suite* matinee and here I was a MoMA, in the midst of a cocktail party, then on my way to the Red Matisse exhibit, Picasso and everything else there was time for.

Art museums always feel like a safe landing. I've been fortunate to visit museums in Paris, Copenhagen, San Francisco, Chicago, Minneapolis and several other cities, including here in New York. A museum is a place to feel comfortably alone, where a solitary woman standing in front of a Matisse attracts zero attention.

That's New York, too. Nobody notices if you're by yourself – a tourist with an iced coffee, perched on a bench in Central Park, her face lifted to the warmth of the midsummer sun, simultaneously surrounded by quiet and noise.

My "social interactions" on this trip were minimal at best. Pleasantries to a server at Café Un Deux Trois, to a barista at the coffee shop near my hotel, to the usher at the Hudson Theatre before taking my seat for the Wednesday matinee.

Surrounded by pockets of people, mostly older women, some with friends, many who had probably made the trip to the theater on the subway, I found myself smiling.

I merely listened while other people talked around me, while SJP and Matthew Broderick talked to each other on stage.

In New York once again, I reveled at being in the midst of a party that was both sprawling and intimate. And now, I look at myself 'backward,' remembering that trip and clearly seeing everything that made it wonderful.

ABOUT THE AUTHOR

After 40 years, Klecko has moved from the Capital City
To Babylon across the river
Where he lives with a rescue dog from San Francisco
Named FiFi who happened to be born
On Christmas Day 2023

www.ingramcontent.com/pod-product-compliance
Lightning Source LLC
Chambersburg PA
CBHW071514120626
46550CB00006B/2224